365
Peaceful Days to Color

Thunder Bay Press
An imprint of Printers Row Publishing Group
10350 Barnes Canyon Road, Suite 100, San Diego, CA 92121
www.thunderbaybooks.com

Copyright © 2016 Quantum Books

Printers Row Publishing Group is a division of Readerlink Distribution Services, LLC. The Thunder Bay Press name and logo are trademarks of Readerlink Distribution Services, LLC.

All notations of errors or omissions should be addressed to Thunder Bay Press, Editorial Department, at the above address. All other correspondence (author inquiries, permissions) concerning the content of this book should be addressed to Quantum Books Ltd at the address below.

Thunder Bay Press
Publisher: Peter Norton
Publishing Team: Lori Asbury, Ana Parker, Laura Vignale, Kathryn Chipinka
Editorial Team: JoAnn Padgett, Melinda Allman, Traci Douglas
Production Team: Jonathan Lopes, Rusty von Dyl

This book was designed, conceived, and produced by Quantum Books Ltd
6 Blundell Street
London, N7 9BH
United Kingdom

Publisher: Kerry Enzor
Managing Editor: Julia Shone
Editorial: Philippa Davis and Nicky Hill
Design: Amazing 15
Production Manager: Zarni Win
With illustrations from Andrew Pinder

ISBN: 978-1-62686-815-1

Printed in China by 1010 Printing International Ltd.

20 19 18 17 16   1 2 3 4 5

365
Peaceful Days to Color

Enjoy calm every day with meditative patterns and mindful affirmations

LONA EVERSDEN

THUNDER BAY
P·R·E·S·S

San Diego, California

"It is wonderful to be me"

"I am so grateful for all my body can do"

"The only place I need to be is right here, right now"

"My mood is light and positive"

Contents

Introduction

In today's busy world, we all need to pause occasionally and gain a sense of peace. Adult coloring is the perfect way to do this.

Research shows that when we color, our breathing becomes deeper, our heart rate slows, our mind quiets down, and time seems to slow. Like meditation, coloring allows us to step into the moment, and so helps our stresses and worries to drift away.

Why is adult coloring so relaxing? It is partly to do with the intricacy and the detail of the designs. They encourage your mind to engage fully with what you are doing, so that all of your thoughts are focused on the task, and you reach a kind of "flow," a mindful state that is inherently relaxing.

Coloring also allows you to express your creative side. Each of us has our own take on how to treat a particular design, from the colors we choose to the symmetry and patterns we create on the page. Coloring is immensely satisfying because it is an activity in which we can instantly see progress— in the sense that the picture moves toward completion and in the sense that we become more skilled with each project we undertake. For many of us, coloring takes us back to one of the simple pleasures of childhood. It reignites the carefree joy in doing something that came to us easily when we were young. It is a great way to remind ourselves that there is time for us to enjoy ourselves, regardless of responsibilities we may have and however busy our lives may be.

This book has been designed to enhance the relaxing and empowering effects of coloring. It offers you a beautiful design for every day of the year. Each image has been specially chosen to induce a sense of happiness or calm, and comes with a powerful affirmation. So turn to the page for today, pick up your pencils, and start your year of mindful coloring.

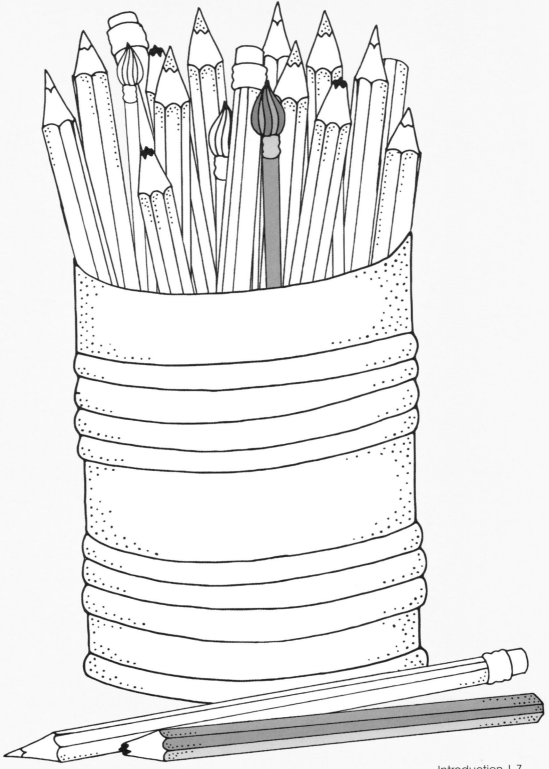

Practicing Mindfulness

Mindfulness means "embracing the moment"—that is, being aware of what is happening right now rather than worrying about the past or the future.

Too often we go about our day on autopilot, barely noticing what we are doing because we are caught up in our thoughts. Research shows a wandering mind makes us feel unhappy and stressed. Conversely, when we engage fully with our moment-by-moment experience we enjoy life more and feel less anxious.

Activities such as coloring, which rest and quiet the mind, are a great way to introduce yourself to a more mindful way of living. It helps to begin each coloring session by spending a few moments being aware of your breathing to calm your mind. Try placing the palms of your hands on your belly. Take a slow, deep breath in, allowing the breath to go all the way down to your belly. Notice how it gently pushes out against your hands, then relaxes as you breathe out. Do this three times, just noticing how it feels to breathe in and out. Then, when you feel ready, begin your coloring.

Using Affirmations

One effect of mindfulness may be that we begin to notice our negative thoughts. Many of us have an inner voice that is harsh and pessimistic. Affirmations are short statements that can help us to change our inner voice to one that is kind and empowering, and thus adopt a more positive attitude toward life.

Each coloring design in this book comes with an inspiring affirmation to transform your day. Some are intended to help you access a calmer state of mind, others build confidence, your creativity, or your sense of joy. Over time, they can help you to rise above stress, live in the moment, be happy, and realize your potential. Here's how to get the most from affirmations:

- **Say Them Often**
  Repeat the day's affirmation several times for a minute or so. Do this before and after you color, and then at intervals throughout the day.

- **Let Go of Judgment**
  Do not worry whether you believe the affirmation. Simply concentrate on repeating the words to yourself.

- **Wait and See**
  Don't ask yourself if the affirmation is working or making a difference to your day. It takes time for your inner voice to change. Just say it without expectation, and see what happens.

Finding an Affirmation

This book is designed to be worked through day by day, but if you have a specific area of well-being that you want to focus on you can turn to the index (see pages 380–383) to find the right affirmation for your needs. In the index the affirmations are listed by subject area so that you can discover the best one to help boost your confidence, focus your mind, or inspire gratitude.

Coloring Essentials

How you color the designs in this book is totally up to you—there are no rules and no restrictions. That's the fun of adult coloring. However, it's best to use colored pencils because these will not bleed through the page as markers do. Pencils also give you a high degree of precision, which is helpful when coloring intricate patterns. And you can vary the level of shading by pressing more lightly or firmly, or by creating layers of color.

There are all sorts of colored pencils available. It's fine to use ordinary children's pencils, or you can buy artist's pencils. Artist's pencils have higher-quality pigment, which makes them smoother to use, blendable, and better for layering. They also tend to have finer points, which is useful for tiny details. Some people like to use watercolor pencils, which are used the same way as a traditional pencil, but then you can brush a little water over the top to create a more painted effect.

Here are some other ways to get the best out of the designs and the time you devote to them.

1. Make Space
Gather everything you need before you start to color: your pencils, sharpener, container for the sharpenings, this book. You may like to create a dedicated coloring space, or to keep your coloring kit in a special box so that everything is easy to find.

2. Be Comfortable
Some people like to color sitting on the sofa or on a bed; others prefer to be at a table. Do whatever feels right for you, but make sure that you feel relaxed and comfortable.

3. Find Time
The great thing about coloring is that you can do it at any time—you might like to get up early in the morning and enjoy some coloring before the rush, or it might be something you do to wind down in the evening. Some people like to color on their commute... whatever suits you is just fine.

4. Create with Color
Don't think too hard about the colors you choose, but let your instincts guide you. You may find that you quite naturally opt for calming colors or inspiring hues that enhance the message of the affirmation—or you may find it fun to make a point of doing this. The choice is yours.

Inspired by Color

On each coloring page a small segment of the design has been colored in to provide inspiration for your own creativity. You can take your cue from the colors used or go in a completely different direction. Allow your mood and instincts to guide your color choice for each image, and see how the colors you use change from day to day, or even within a design.

How to Use This Book

This book is designed to give you a whole year of peaceful, mindful coloring, with one beautiful design for every day of the year. Each image has been specially chosen to encourage mindful coloring, and comes with an affirmation that complements the design.

Turn to today's page—whether that is January 1st or any other day in the year. Read the affirmation and spend a few moments thinking about what that means to you. Then enjoy unwinding, de-stressing, and expressing yourself through the power and beauty of color.

For those times when you want to focus on a specific area of well-being, you can use the index of affirmations on pages 380–383 to find affirmations by topic, whether you need a quick confidence boost or a mantra to help you relax from worries.

A Peaceful Year

Whether you are starting on January 1st, June 7th, or December 20th, turn to the relevant page in this book and begin your peaceful year.

Enjoy carving out a quiet moment every day through the mindful practice of coloring. Use this time to focus on your own needs and your personal well-being. Reflect on the affirmation for that day—be it about inspiring confidence, promoting calm, or expressing gratitude—and use these mantras to help you discover a more tranquil way of life.

January 1

I choose to be happy.

January 2

Each new day is full of undreamed possibilities.

January 3

Only when I let go do I see how far I can rise.

January 4

I greet each morning invigorated and ready to start a new day.

January 5

I face my fears with the strength and courage of a lion.

January 6

Energy flows through every part of my body, and I feel invigorated.

January 7

My talents are blossoming, transforming my life in unexpected ways.

Ianuary 8

Magical things happen when I focus my energy on what I love most.

January 9

Today I set my mind to complete every task with the passion it deserves.

January 10

I know that I am worth all the good things in my life,
and that many more are coming to me.

January 11

I take pride in both my body and my mind, knowing that
beauty is about more than appearance.

January 12

When I am feeling down, I look up to the sky and
remember that the world is a big place full of opportunity.

January 13

My happiness is my responsibility and no one else's.

January 14

There is always a way through—even when the path seems full of obstacles.

January 15

My community is full of people who have hopes and fears, just like me.

January 16

I am the star of my life and I shine in all I do.

January 17

Every day opens a door to new adventures.

January 18

I accept with thanks the small gifts that others offer me—
a smile, a helping hand, a sympathetic ear.

January 19

I sail my own way, however choppy the waves may be.

January 20

The independent, creative spirit of Aquarius the water-carrier flows through me.

January 21

I have clear goals in mind and I work hard to achieve them.

January 22

I glow with contentment and good health.

January 23

I release old grudges and open my heart to compassion and understanding.

January 24

My inner self is calm and peaceful.

January 25

I forgive the past and move on from it.

Janaury 26

I am as unique and beautiful as a snowflake.

January 27

Today I carry kindness in my heart and express it through my voice;
I speak as sweetly as the birds sing.

January 28

When I don't know where to start I remember that
starting anywhere is better than not starting at all.

January 29

I approach my day with an attitude of gratitude.

January 30

I trust my instincts and follow my heart.

January 31

I conserve my energy for when I need it most.

February 1

The harsher the winds that buffet me, the deeper my roots grow.

February 2

Through forgiveness comes freedom.

February 3

I have the wisdom to know when to keep my own counsel.

February 4

Just as every oak tree grows from an acorn, so each
great achievement starts from small beginnings.

February 5

I use my intelligence to come up with innovative ideas. I am a creative thinker.

February 6

My instincts are my guiding light in everything that I do.

February 7

I have the courage to believe in the beauty of my dreams.

February 8

Every day I take time to pause and reflect on all the wonderful things in my life.

February 9

Focusing on each breath, I find the stillness within myself.

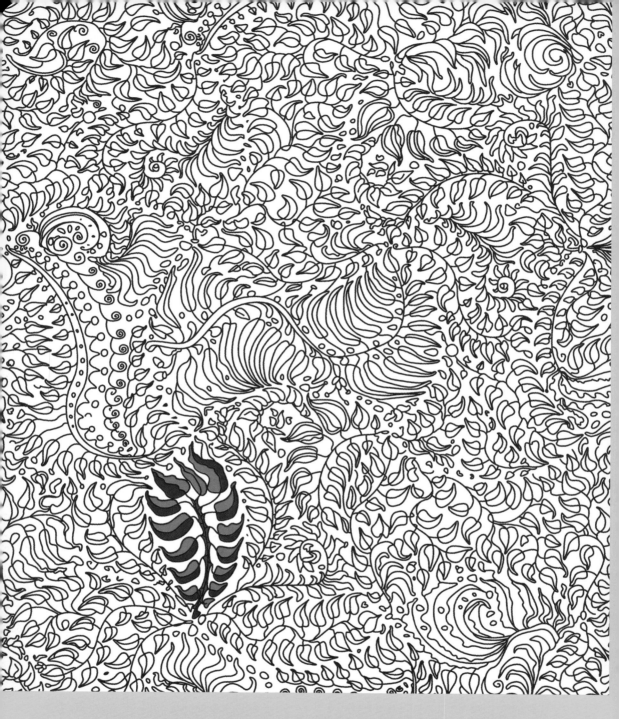

February 10

I celebrate the beauty in every exquisite detail of our
world, from a falling leaf to the shape of a smile.

February 11

Like the butterfly, I am free to follow my dreams.

February 12

I have broken free from old habits, and I am moving on in my life.

February 13

Today I am positive in everything I think, say, and do.

February 14

I am open to the unknown and accept that
some outcomes are outside of my control.

February 15

Everywhere I look, I see the miracle of life.

February 16

I keep my cool however heated others become.

February 17

I am the embodiment of grace.

February 18

I am protected and safe.

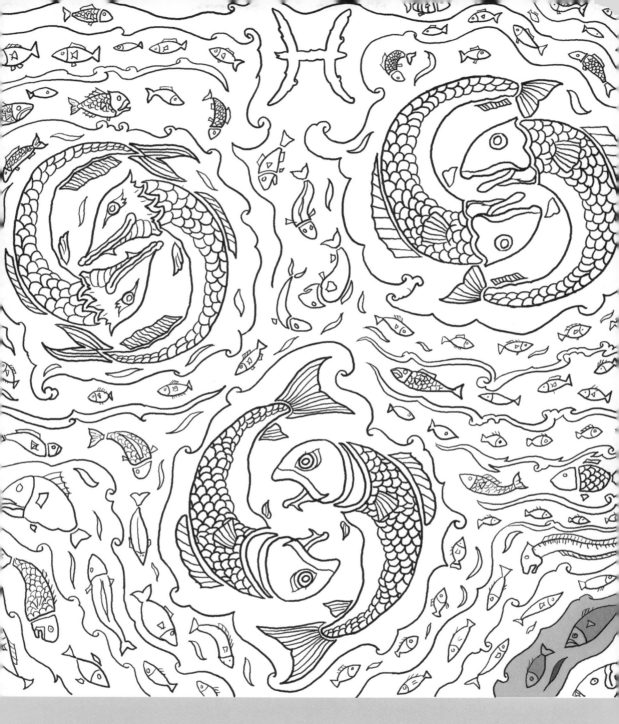

February 19

Like Pisces the fish, I can swim with the current or against it,
and I make the most of any situation I find myself in.

February 20

Whatever challenges the day brings, I can handle them.

February 21

I bring a sense of spaciousness to my day.

February 22

I stay in the present moment, knowing that it is filled with riches.

February 23

I nurture my body and soul with deep, meaningful rest.

February 24

I observe my emotions calmly, as if through the dispassionate lens of the camera.

February 25

I welcome the sun into my day, and allow its healing
light to infuse everything that I do.

February 26

Today, a river of creative energy flows within me
unleashing a torrent of great ideas.

February 27

Even in difficult times, there is always a beacon of light guiding me forward.

February 28

I treat my body with kindness at all times.

February 29

I embrace new opportunities with excitement.

March 1

I am a natural decision maker; I make the right choices at the right time.

March 2

I believe it and then achieve it!

March 3

The key to realizing my potential is confidence in my own abilities.

March 4

I leave my work at work; at home, I embrace relaxation.

March 5

I take a little time each day to daydream.

March 6

I live in harmony with those around me.

March 7

I honor the joy of life; I allow it to transport me to happier places.

March 8

My breath is my anchor; at any time I can use
it to reconnect to the present moment.

March 9

I make the most of life's sweetest moments.

March 10

I am always open to new ideas.

March 11

Every decision I make creates exciting new possibilities in my life.

March 12

I welcome times of solitude and enjoy my own company.

March 13

I am happy when others succeed, knowing that there is enough for all of us.

March 14

I bring serenity to every situation I find myself in.

March 15

Today, I broaden my awareness and notice the positive
changes that are already happening in my life.

March 16

I realize I cannot know what the day brings;
I only know to expect the unexpected.

March 17

I maintain a little place of quiet inside myself,
and know that I can go there at any point.

March 18

I choose to be with friends who know, accept, and love the real me.

March 19

I am at peace with my past, my present, and my future.

March 20

I freely express my thanks for all that I receive today.

March 21

Like Aries, the ram, I will throw myself headlong into
the day and tackle all tasks with enthusiasm and optimism.

March 22

My love for my family manifests itself in kind acts and words.

March 23

All the threads of my life are woven together in one wonderful tapestry.

March 24

I appreciate the support and comfort that I receive from others.

March 25

I choose to act with confidence.

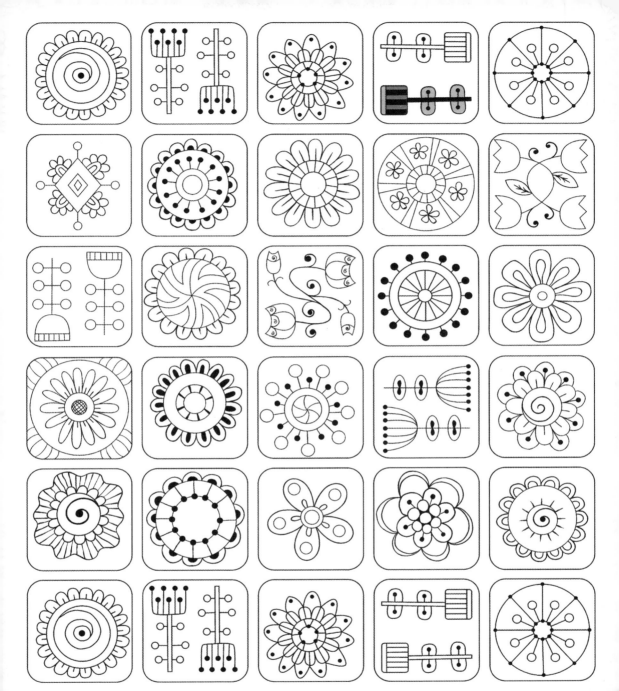

March 26

I bring positivity into everything I say and do.

March 27

I am willing to let go of my worries;
I ease myself into a more relaxed way of being.

March 28

I embrace the changes that are occurring in my life,
and have faith that they are in my best interest.

March 29

I navigate unknown situations with ease.

March 30

I am not afraid to go against the tide.

March 31

My focus is on what truly matters.

April 1

I am at peace with my surroundings.

April 2

I follow my dreams and take steps to make them my reality.

April 3

I see the good in everyone I meet today.

April 4

Everywhere I turn I see a reason to smile.

April 5

I cherish the time I spend in my home.

April 6

I practice gratitude every day and thankfulness becomes my melody.

April 7

It is enough to be myself.

April 8

My life is rich with blessings and I am thankful for each one.

April 9

I feel invigorated and alive, full of energy for everything I want to do.

april 10

I remember the good things that others
have done for me and I let go of the misdeeds.

April 11

When people speak to me, I listen with mindful attention.

April 12

Just as the lotus flower rises above the water, so I rise above
my difficulties and turn my face to the light.

April 13

I breathe in peace and breathe out love.

April 14

Every moment is a new beginning.

April 15

I have faith in my ability to provide for myself and for my family.

April 16

Amazing things happen when you believe in the possibilities of your imagination.

April 17

I am naturally optimistic; I look for the silver lining in every cloud.

April 18

My cares feel as light as the air; I watch them float away.

April 19

The world is a garden of ideas and I delight in each new discovery.

April 20

I grab every situation by the horns. I have the bravery
of Taurus the bull and I stand up for myself.

April 21

I embrace my flaws, knowing that perfection is an illusion.

April 22

There is abundance everywhere; I have everything I need and more.

April 23

I believe that I deserve success, and I am prepared to work hard to achieve it.

April 24

I go lightly through my day, trusting that I will find what I need whenever I need it.

April 25

I can open the gate to happiness at any moment.

April 26

I am a fun-loving person with a playful side.

April 27

I wake up feeling happy and full of energy.

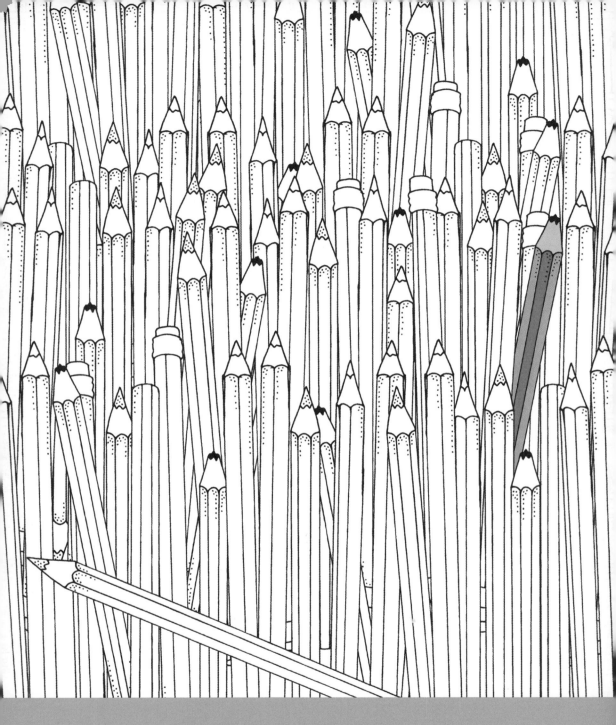

April 28

Coloring is my way of finding a few precious moments of peace.

April 29

Every day I seize the opportunity to learn something new.

April 30

I am strong and powerful enough to make choices that suit who I am.

May 1

I acknowledge and appreciate the support and love of my friends and family.

May 2

My creative energy is a fountain of brilliant ideas.

May 3

Though I may pass through periods of difficulty,
I remember that these are only a small part of life.

May 4

I have the confidence to let my sparkle show.

May 5

I shed old beliefs that no longer serve me.
I am not who I was as a child; I have grown.

May 6

Fear does not stop me; great courage lies within me
and I know I can draw on it at any moment.

May 7

From my mistakes come opportunities.

May 8

I give my whole heart to my purpose in life.

May 9

On every hour, I pause and breathe.

May 10

Like the bright sunflower, I raise my face to the sun and give thanks for the opportunity to grow.

May 11

I visualize what I want to achieve and make it a reality.

May 12

Today I blaze a trail through my world.

May 13

I create a happy and calm environment; my home is my sanctuary.

May 14

I stand tall and let my inner worth reveal itself.

May 15

Love and peace are at the center of my being.

May 16

My sense of tranquility expresses itself in everything I do.

May 17

My inner voice is gentle; I speak to myself with love.

May 18

There is always time for love and nurture.

May 19

I have complete freedom to do what I want and go where I like.

May 20

I am attracting love and affection into my life.

May 21

Like Gemini, the twins, I am able to see both sides
of any situation and I am open to new experiences.

May 22

My home is a cozy, safe place to be.

May 23

I take great pleasure in small indulgences.

May 24

I focus on taking one step at a time, trusting that
I am moving toward my highest goal.

May 25

Today I choose to make changes not excuses.

May 26

I love to switch off all electronic devices and spend a few minutes in silence.

May 27

I have the courage to ask for help when I need it, and know that I can rely on my family and friends to support me.

May 28

I rise like the sun, full of energy and brightness.

May 29

Each day I bring a little holiday happiness into my life.

May 30

I am full of appreciation for everything that my body allows me to do.

May 31

Laughter comes easily to me; I make time to laugh every day.

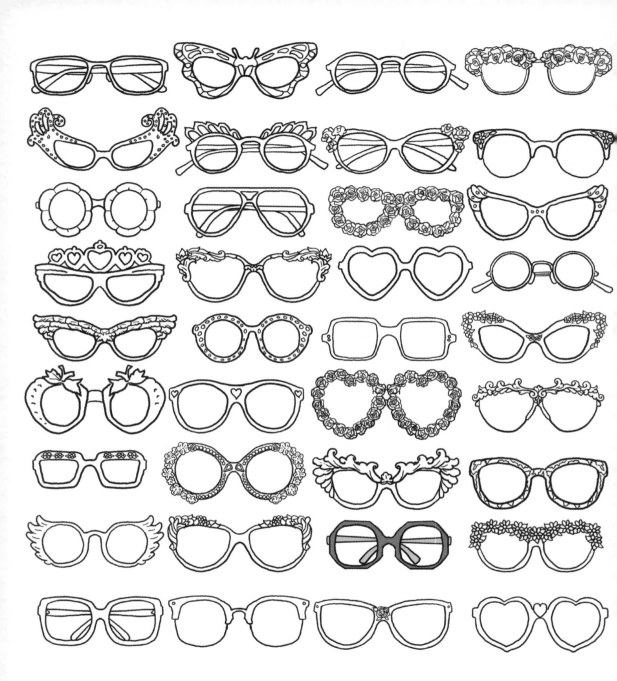

June 1

I always look on the bright side; I am a natural optimist.

June 2

I love the sense of connection that I feel with other people.

June 3

One step at a time is all it takes for me to move along my path.

June 4

When I have something to say, I express it calmly and freely.

June 5

I radiate goodwill to everyone I meet.

June 6

Wonderful things are drawn to me.

June 7

My smile is radiant with joy.

June 8

My heart is open. I give out love and love is given to me.

June 9

I am grateful for all the good things that are sent my way.

June 10

I find happiness everywhere I choose to see it.

June 11

In times of darkness, I look up at the stars and
remind myself that there is always light.

June 12

I am conquering the obstacles that block my
way and creating a happier, better life.

June 13

I do not strive to be perfect because I accept myself for who I am.

June 14

Everything I experience, positive or negative,
increases my potential for growth.

June 15

I prioritize the most important tasks of my day and proceed with clarity.

June 16

I am constantly growing in mind and spirit.

June 17

I release my fears and watch them fly away.

June 18

I choose confidence. I have faith in my ability to succeed.

June 19

I am a strong person and I offer support to those around me.

June 20

My confidence is blossoming and I know my future is full of promise.

June 21

Cancer, the crab, is self-sufficient—and the same is true of me.
I feel protected by who I am.

June 22

Every day has its treasure, even if it is hidden from view.

June 23

My relationships are loving and lasting.

June 24

I can do it. Yes, I can!

June 25

Being cheerful comes naturally to me. I find it easy
to experience the happiness that the day has to offer.

June 26

I choose what I want from life. Everything I wish for is available to me.

June 27

I create deep emotional bonds with my family and friends.

June 28

I am not afraid to take leaps of faith and follow my heart.

June 29

I treat others with gentleness, and I am equally tender to myself.

June 30

I relinquish my desire to change the past. As I let go
of regrets, I embrace the reality of the now.

July 1

I am radiant. I am blessed with good health and vitality.

July 2

My time is precious and I spend it wisely.

July 3

Today, I bring light into every situation.

July 4

There are quiet places amidst the noise and haste of every day.

July 5

The abundance of the universe is drawn to me in a constant flow of gifts.

July 6

My confidence soars as I learn to appreciate the beauty in myself.

July 7

Inspired by the sensitive deer, I handle conflict with grace and empathy.

July 8

Every act of love or kindness makes the world a happier place.

July 9

All is well in my world.

July 10

I am perfectly in tune with myself and my needs.

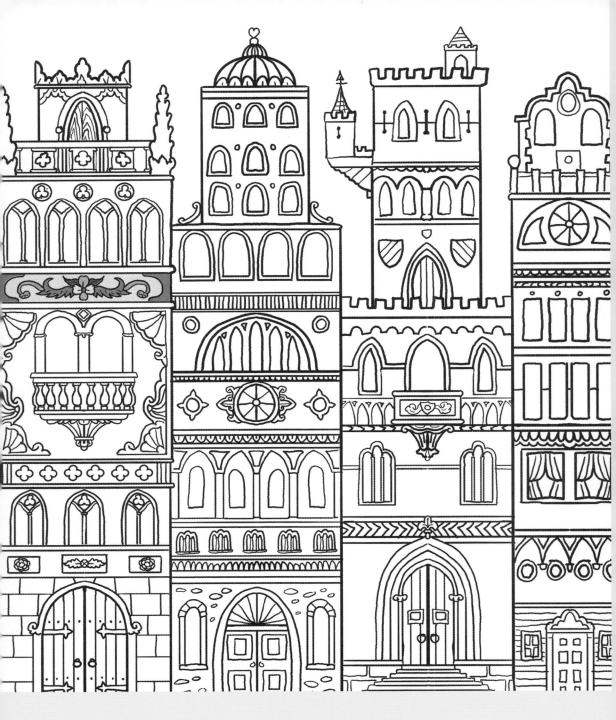

July 11

I am the architect of my own life, and I choose to make it magical.

July 12

I am grateful to all those who have been my teachers.
They have illuminated my world.

July 13

Everything is coming together as it should.

July 14

I am nurtured by the beauty of the world around me.

July 15

Inspiration comes to me from many different directions; I am energized by my day.

July 16

Each day I take some time to just be. I allow my
thoughts to drift past like falling feathers.

July 17

I have a place inside myself where I can
take refuge; all I need to do is breathe.

July 18

There is a deep well of compassion within me;
I draw from it whenever I need to.

July 19

I am a truthful and honorable person.

July 20

I am so relaxed. Tension melts away as I release my worries.

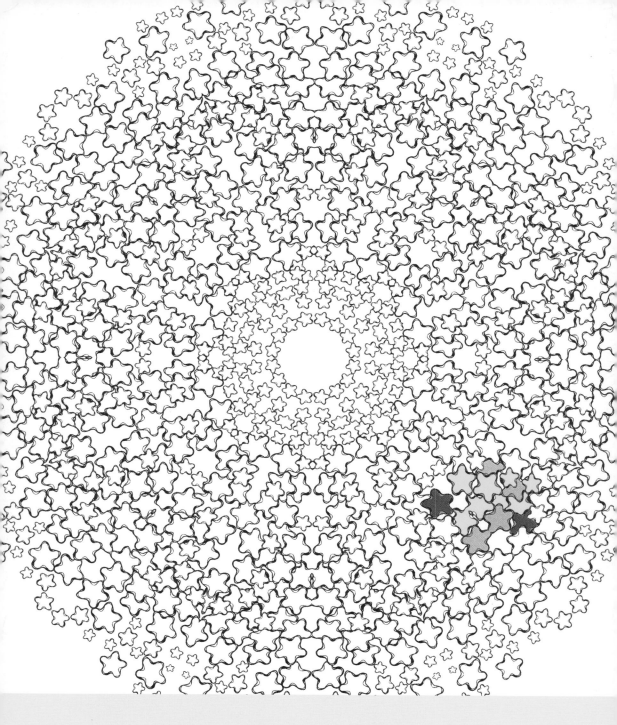

July 21

The blessings in my life are boundless, like the stars in the heavens.

July 22

I am in charge of my own destiny.

July 23

There is a force within me that is as strong as Leo, the lion.
I own that power and it moves me forward.

July 24

I am organized and in control. My mind is focused.

July 25

My needs are just as important as those of everyone around me.

July 26

My life is filled with love.

July 27

I am flexible in my thinking. I take time to
listen to others and learn from them.

July 28

Like a cat, I am astute and resourceful.
I have the ability to adapt to new situations.

July 29

Wherever I look, I see joy.

July 30

I find it easy to work in total harmony with others.

July 31

Good luck always comes my way. I am so fortunate to have what I have.

August 1

Being creative is a key part of who I am. I create beautiful things.

August 2

I allow the possibility that today may be very different than I imagine.
I recognize my expectations are merely thoughts.

August 3

I have a natural wisdom that helps me to
understand the truth of any situation.

August 4

I celebrate my uniqueness.

August 5

In the face of adversity, I display the dignity and strength of the tiger.

August 6

I adore my body and know that beauty comes in all shapes and sizes.

August 7

A sense of peace flows effortlessly through me.

August 8

I hold the key to my own happiness.

August 9

I love the fact that we are all so different,
yet all so wonderful in our own way.

August 10

My ability to conquer challenges is limitless;
my potential to thrive is infinite.

August 11

I am worthy of love just the way I am.

August 12

My life is already transformed; I open my mind and
notice the marvelous changes in my everyday world.

August 13

I have love and respect for all living things.

August 14

At the end of the day I embrace deep, restful sleep in a field of dreams.

August 15

There is no limit to my happiness.

August 16

My heart sings with passion.

august 17

My life feels balanced and peaceful right now.

August 18

Today I proceed with clarity and conviction.

August 19

There is such pleasure to be had in the
simple affection I share with others.

August 20

I have respect for the deep wisdom that lies within me.
When I receive a flash of inspiration, I act on it.

August 21

Healing energy is flowing through me.

August 22

Everything I undertake bears fruit in a beautiful way.

August 23

Today I honor the warmth and generosity of the maiden
Virgo by being a kind and thoughtful friend.

august 24

I am grateful to belong to such a wonderful
community of people. We look out for each other.

August 25

A little time to let my mind wander allows
my creativity and imagination to flourish.

August 26

Life is sweet. Life is full of wonder. My dreams can come true.

August 27

I shape my own future.

August 28

Every day I create a sense of beauty in my life.

August 29

I am working to achieve the results that I want.

August 30

I know that I can go higher, and then higher still.

August 31

I see beauty in my friends, my colleagues, and in all those around me.

September 1

My calm approach means that potential conflicts
become productive discussions.

September 2

I am happy, vital, enthusiastic—and glad to be alive!

September 3

I maintain my equilibrium in whatever storms the day may bring.

September 4

Thank you world, for all that you give me and all that you are.

September 5

I feel the love of those who are no longer with me and am comforted.

September 6

I listen to those I can trust.

September 7

I nurture my creative self by doing something artistic every day.

September 8

I live in harmony with the world around me.

September 9

Like the seahorse, I hold my place and remain
calm, even with turbulent currents around me.

September 10

At any moment I can tap into the source of great
energy that is within me and feel revitalized and strong.

September 11

Life is full of adventure. There are always
new things to try and new places to go.

September 12

I chart my way across clear waters. I am on course.

September 13

When I nurture my ideas, I see them grow.

September 14

My work fulfills me, and I am good at what I do.

September 15

When I want something to happen, I express my
desire for it and I trust that it will all unfold before me.

September 16

I am highly productive in every area of my life.

September 17

Though I may be working hard below the surface,
I present a serene vision of myself to the world.

September 18

I treat myself with the loving kindness and
gentle forgiveness that I deserve.

September 19

All I have to do to make today perfect is smile!

September 20

Having happy thoughts brings more joy into my life.

September 21

My life is filled with magic. My wishes are manifesting into reality.

September 22

Learning new things is important to me;
I love to feed my mind with knowledge.

September 23

Libra, the scales, are a picture of fairness and balance. Today I will be just and even-handed in my dealings with others.

September 24

I have a logical mind; I am able to come up with
clear solutions to any problems that I face.

September 25

I create a sense of home and belonging wherever I go.

September 26

I am thankful for the prosperity and abundance in my life.

September 27

I recognize what brings me true delight and make room for it in my life.

September 28

I allow my doubts to be washed away by a wave of self-belief.

September 29

I express my artistic side in all that I do.

September 30

I have the confidence to show the real me;
I do not need to hide behind a mask.

October 1

I have beautiful things in my home.
I make sure to have beauty around me.

October 2

Everything is under control; I achieve my targets one by one.

October 3

I have faith that life is taking me in the right direction.

October 4

Positive energy flows through my body, bringing joy to every step I take.

October 5

I gather strength from my roots and keep on growing.

October 6

I have the freedom to go my own way, whatever others may do.

October 7

The unconditional love I receive is a wonderful gift in my life.

October 8

Everything I need comes to me at the right time.

October 9

I am an optimistic person and always carry hope with me.

October 10

I have patience with my family and friends, and
acknowledge the love that lies behind their actions.

October 11

One day at a time is enough for me. There is no rush.

October 12

A little bit of nothing time makes me happy.

October 13

Boundless energy is available for me to draw on.

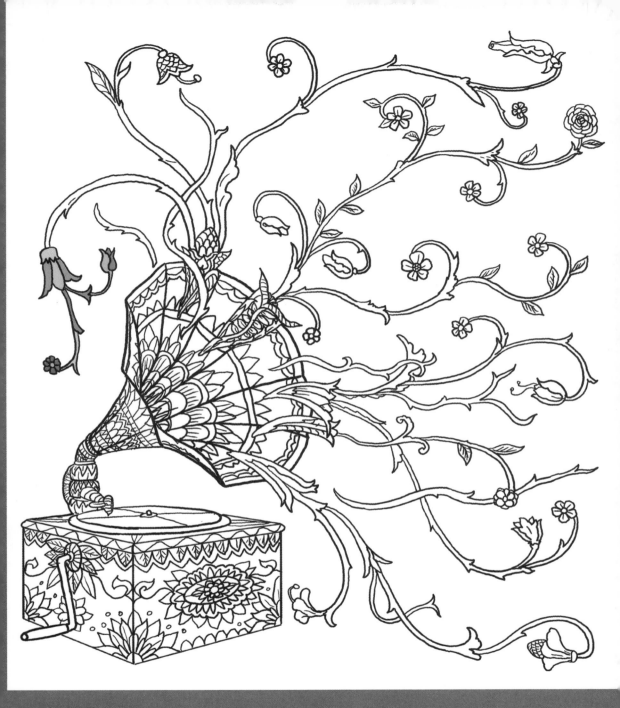

October 14

I unstintingly share the joys in my life with everyone around me.

October 15

I send kind thoughts to all those who need them.

October 16

I am connected to my inner self.
Everything I do reflects the beautiful person I am.

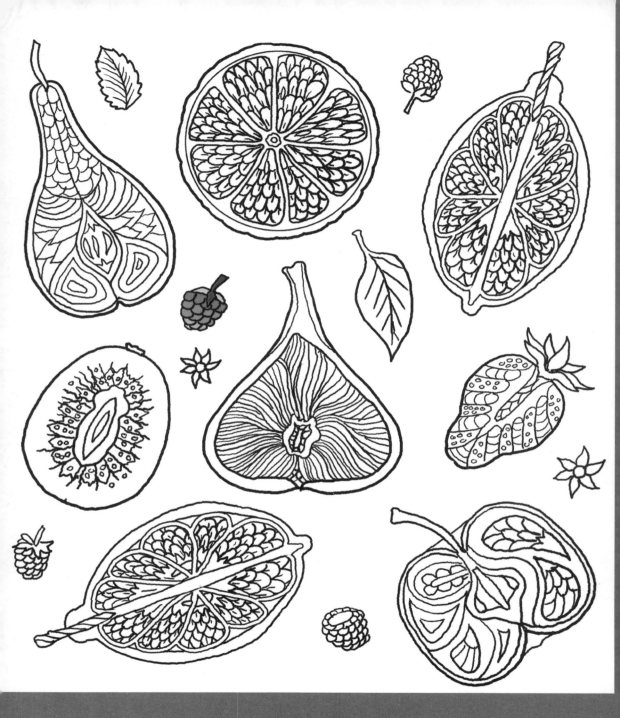

October 17

All my hopes and dreams are coming to fruition.

October 18

I nourish my body with good food, exercise, and plenty of rest.

October 19

In all that I do, I am sowing the seeds of my own future.

October 20

I invite my intuitive self to take charge. I value my instincts.

October 21

Today's gift is absolute clarity of mind. I see everything clearly.

October 22

I love the way I look today.

October 23

The dynamic, passionate energy of Scorpio,
the scorpion, is my driving force today.

October 24

I invite new opportunities into my life.

October 25

I see the good in others. I attract positive people into my life.

October 26

Everyone I meet has something to share; the greatest
lessons can come from the most unlikely teachers.

October 27

I can let go because I have complete confidence in my abilities.

October 28

I allow others to go their own direction. I celebrate freedom for all.

October 29

Every ending is also a new beginning.

October 30

I drink deeply of life's rich experiences.

October 31

I am patient and resilient; I get what I want.

November 1

I choose to do my best. I do not need to compete with others.

November 2

I willingly go with the flow of life.

November 3

I embrace who I am and all my imperfections.

November 4

My fears are drifting away. I am full of hope.

November 5

Every day I wake with a sense of excitement.

November 6

Life is about more than work and money; I take time out to enjoy myself.

November 7

I am moving forward—I am on my way to the life of my dreams.

November 8

I draw inspiration from the incredible beauty of the natural world.

November 9

Loyalty is part of who I am. I show how much I value those I love.

November 10

I have nothing to prove: I am who I am.

November 11

I will make peace with those who have been a source of conflict to me.

November 12

I take good care of myself. I am self-sufficient.

November 13

My ability to adapt to new circumstances is remarkable; I embrace the natural transitions that are occurring in my life.

November 14

I have great patience. I trust that everything is unfolding in the right way.

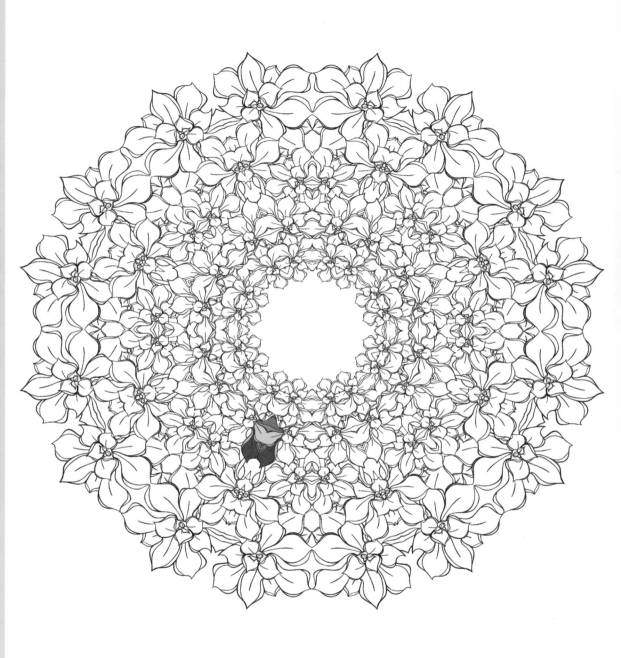

November 15

I release the urge to judge and criticize others
and accept people the way they are.

November 16

Each moment is precious. I organize my life so
that I have time to do what is important to me.

November 17

I open my arms wide and say "yes" to the day
and all the experiences that are in store for me.

November 18

I choose cooperation when working with others.
Although I value my own achievements, I love being part of a team.

November 19

I am richly rewarded for my talents.

November 20

There is a rich and beautiful pattern to my life.
I see the good in what I am doing.

November 21

I move with grace and ease in every step.

November 22

Like Sagittarius, the sharp-eyed archer,
I aim high and true in everything that I undertake.

November 23

I acknowledge the many great qualities that I possess.

November 24

My troubles are melting away, like snowflakes in the sunshine.

November 25

I take care of the things I can control and
trust that the rest will take care of itself.

November 26

I love who I am now, and recognize
that I am always learning and developing.

November 27

I emanate contentment and calm.

November 28

What I do is worthwhile. I make a difference to the world.

November 29

I create my own opportunities, and I persevere until I achieve my aim.

November 30

I love to explore and seek out the many adventures life has to offer.

December 1

There is beauty in even the smallest things.
I am so fortunate to experience it.

December 2

Even in the darkest days, there is hope and the promise of change.

December 3

However challenging my day, there is always time
to step away and savor a moment of peace.

December 4

Success is blooming in all aspects of my life.

December 5

I am completely satisfied with who I am.

December 6

I am in control of my life and choose the direction I travel in.

December 7

I am a master of versatility. I adapt to new circumstances with ease.

December 8

The world is a beautiful place; I am lucky to be here.

December 9

When I feel overwhelmed, I allow myself time for rest and recuperation.

December 10

Each day, I take a moment to check in with
my body and my own needs. I nurture myself.

December 11

I feel completely secure at all times.

December 12

I have fun and appreciate the joys of life.

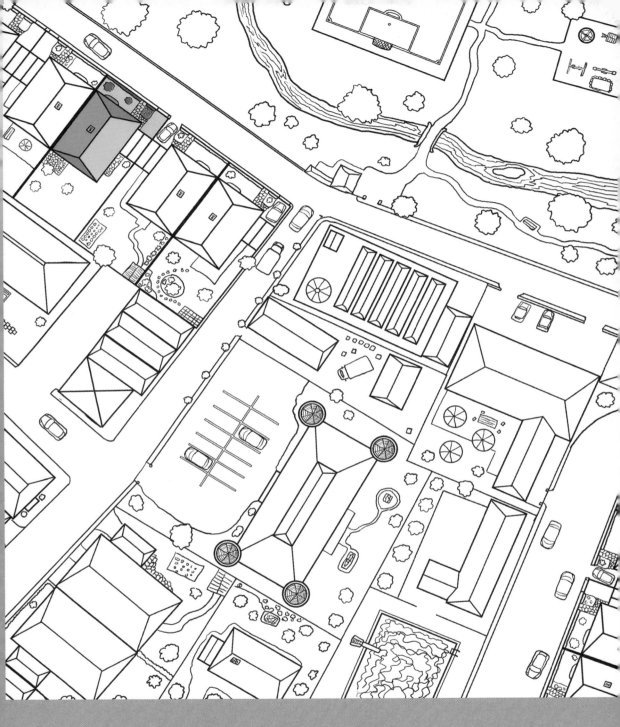

December 13

I am a flexible thinker—I am always able to look
at situations from a new angle.

December 14

Forgiveness is a gift, and I know that I am deserving of it.

December 15

Every day, I simplify my life to focus on the things that matter most.

December 16

I respect others and they respect me.

December 17

My inner wisdom lights my way.

December 18

I am true to myself.

December 19

I get what I want from life because I communicate my needs clearly.

December 20

I belong! I feel so happy about my place in the world.

December 21

When I am thankful for what I have, my worries lessen or disappear.

December 22

Inspired by Capricorn, the mountain goat,
I am sure of my footing—and I persevere.

December 23

I am content with my present and full of hope for the future.

December 24

What goes around comes around. I do good in
the world and I receive good back many times over.

December 25

Joy illuminates my day.

December 26

My life is a perfect balance between
doing and being, giving and receiving.

December 27

I give myself the space I need to grow.

December 28

The sweetest things in life are given freely and gladly.

December 29

I am friendly and playful, and do not take myself too seriously.

December 30

I honor my own needs.

December 31

I am moving into a more joyous way of living.

Index

Acknowledgments

Quantum Books would like to thank the following for supplying images for inclusion in this book:

Special thanks to **Andrew Pinder** for his beautiful and unique artwork: Cover illustrations

Page 12 (lower left and top right); Page 13 (top and right); January 1, 2, 3, 4, 8, 14, 20, 22, 26; February 1, 5, 6, 7, 12, 13, 16, 18, 19, 26, 27; March 3, 14, 19, 21; April 5, 8, 9, 12, 16, 20, 24, 25, 26, 29; May 1, 2, 3, 4, 9, 12, 18, 19, 21, 22, 24, 25, 27, 28; June 1, 3, 7, 11, 21, 22, 26; July 2, 3, 4, 6, 10, 11, 12, 17, 18, 21, 23, 30; August 1, 8, 10, 11, 14, 22, 23, 27; September 3, 6, 12, 13, 17, 18, 21, 23, 25; October 3, 4, 14, 17, 19, 23, 27, 28; November 4, 5, 22, 25, 29, 30; December 12, 13, 22, 24, 25, 26, 31

Shutterstock.com

Alena Dubinets February 24
Alfadanz July 28; October 31
Alka5051 January 11; September 9
Anastasia Evseneva February 3; July 31
Andriy Lipkan June 2
Balabolka February 20; September 28
Big Boy August 20, 29; October 15
Bimbim Page 11; April 14; May 8, 23, 30; June 12, 25; August 13; September 5; October 10; December 6, 7
Bimbim (vitasunny) May 20
Catherine Glazkova December 19
Cerama_ama January 16, 18; September 10; November 23; December 20
Curiosity December 16
Emila October 1
Evgeniya Anfimova Page 12 (left); October 20
Exclusivelly March 23
Franzi June 30
Fricke Studio March 2
FuzzyLogicKate November 7
Gala Matorina Page 4 (second row right); Page 5 (second row)
Galina Shpak Page 4 (top row middle, second row left, third row left and right); Page 5 (top and third row)
Hanna kutsybala May 5; August 6 (top left and top right). November 9
Helen Lane June 6 (middle), 17, 23 (middle); December 14
HikaruD88 May 16; November 15
Imagepluss January 10, 27; March 25, 31; April 10; July 7, 8, 25; August 16; September 1; December 9
ImHope Page 7; January 15, 17, 19, 25, 28; February 4, 14, 21, 22, 23; March 13, 20; April 18, 19, 28; May 10; June 9, 10, 13, 16, 20, 24, 27; July 5, 26; August 2, 18; September 22; October 5, 9, 21; November 2; December 3, 17
IR Stone January 12; June 19
IrinaKrivoruchko Page 1; January 29, 30; March 27; April 11, 23, 30; May 7; June 6 (surround); July 1, 15; August 4; September 2, 15, 27; November 10, 13; December 15
Ivala January 24; April 15
Julia Snegireva January 6; March 26; April 7; May 11, 31; June 18; July 20; August 9, 28; September 11, 16, 29; October 7, 8, 18, 22, 24; November 27; December 4, 5, 8
Karakotsya March 12; May 13
Kchungtw May 6
Kochkanyan Juliya October 26
Kurilenko Katya February 8
L. Kramer February 10; April 3
Lexver March 6, 18; July 29
Lidia Puica December 28
Lolla Lenn Page 8
Lolya1988 May 17
Mamita June 28
Maryna S May 26
Mashabr Page 12 (left); January 7, 13; February 15; March 5, 9; June 14; August 12; September 14; October 25; November 14, 17
Mis-Tery September 7; December 21
Nadezhda Molkentin July 13, 14; September 30; October 11; November 18
Nuttapol January 5
Oksanka007 Page 2 (right); February 2; May 14, 15; June 15, 23; September 5; October 6; November 19; December 2, 23, Page 383
Olesia Agudova Page 2 (left); Page 3; April 1; August 24; November 28
Olga Zakharova August 26
OlichO February 25; March 1, 15, 16, 17, 22; April 13, 21, 27; July 22, 24; August 7; September 4, 19; December 27
Paket February 9
Palomita March 11; June 4
Panki Page 4 (top row right, lower row left and right); Page 5 (lower); Page 12 (middle); February 29; April 17; June 8, 29; August 6 (middle right), 19, 30; September 26; October 7
Photo-nuke March 24; November 21, 24; December 1
Rita Gennari March 10
Roman Poijak August 5
Sablegear February 28; June 5; July 9, 16; August 17, 26
Scotch-me December 11
Sliplee July 27; August 21; September 20; October 2, 13, 29; November 1
Son80 December 29
Snezh January 21
Toporovska Natalila January 24; April 22; May 29; August 15; November 26
TotallyPic.com January 31; February 11; March 28, 30; April 4; August 3; December 10
Uni Ula October 30; November 20
Uvlek April 6; November 8, 16
Vasylieva Yuliya August 6 (lower left)
Vareennik February 17
Victor Z January 9
Vitasunny March 4; October 16; December 18, 30
Watercolor-swallow March 7, 8, 29; April 2; July 19; November 11
YAZZIK November 6
YoPizArt November 12
Zelena September 24; November 3